A declaration of the true manner of knowing Christ crucified (1611)

William Perkins

A declaration of the true manner of knowing Christ crucified
Perkins, William, 1558-1602.
Dedication signed: W. Perkins.
Running title: Of the right knowledge of Christ crucified.
Identified as STC 19686a on UMI microfilm.
[2], 70 p.
Printed at London : By Iohn Legate, printer to the Vniuersitie of Cambridge. 1611. And are to be sold in Pauls Churchyard at the signe of the Crowne by Simon Waterson, [1611]
STC (2nd ed.) / 19686.5
English
Reproduction of the original in the Folger Shakespeare Library

Early English Books Online (EEBO) Editions

Imagine holding history in your hands.

Now you can. Digitally preserved and previously accessible only through libraries as Early English Books Online, this rare material is now available in single print editions. Thousands of books written between 1475 and 1700 and ranging from religion to astronomy, medicine to music, can be delivered to your doorstep in individual volumes of high-quality historical reproductions.

We have been compiling these historic treasures for more than 70 years. Long before such a thing as "digital" even existed, ProQuest founder Eugene Power began the noble task of preserving the British Museum's collection on microfilm. He then sought out other rare and endangered titles, providing unparalleled access to these works and collaborating with the world's top academic institutions to make them widely available for the first time. This project furthers that original vision.

These texts have now made the full journey -- from their original printing-press versions available only in rare-book rooms to online library access to new single volumes made possible by the partnership between artifact preservation and modern printing technology. A portion of the proceeds from every book sold supports the libraries and institutions that made this collection possible, and that still work to preserve these invaluable treasures passed down through time.

This is history, traveling through time since the dawn of printing to your own personal library.

Initial Proquest EEBO Print Editions collections include:

Early Literature

This comprehensive collection begins with the famous Elizabethan Era that saw such literary giants as Chaucer, Shakespeare and Marlowe, as well as the introduction of the sonnet. Traveling through Jacobean and Restoration literature, the highlight of this series is the Pollard and Redgrave 1475-1640 selection of the rarest works from the English Renaissance.

Early Documents of World History

This collection combines early English perspectives on world history with documentation of Parliament records, royal decrees and military documents that reveal the delicate balance of Church and State in early English government. For social historians, almanacs and calendars offer insight into daily life of common citizens. This exhaustively complete series presents a thorough picture of history through the English Civil War.

Historical Almanacs

Historically, almanacs served a variety of purposes from the more practical, such as planting and harvesting crops and plotting nautical routes, to predicting the future through the movements of the stars. This collection provides a wide range of consecutive years of "almanacks" and calendars that depict a vast array of everyday life as it was several hundred years ago.

Early History of Astronomy & Space

Humankind has studied the skies for centuries, seeking to find our place in the universe. Some of the most important discoveries in the field of astronomy were made in these texts recorded by ancient stargazers, but almost as impactful were the perspectives of those who considered their discoveries to be heresy. Any independent astronomer will find this an invaluable collection of titles arguing the truth of the cosmic system.

Early History of Industry & Science

Acting as a kind of historical Wall Street, this collection of industry manuals and records explores the thriving industries of construction; textile, especially wool and linen; salt; livestock; and many more.

Early English Wit, Poetry & Satire

The power of literary device was never more in its prime than during this period of history, where a wide array of political and religious satire mocked the status quo and poetry called humankind to transcend the rigors of daily life through love, God or principle. This series comments on historical patterns of the human condition that are still visible today.

Early English Drama & Theatre

This collection needs no introduction, combining the works of some of the greatest canonical writers of all time, including many plays composed for royalty such as Queen Elizabeth I and King Edward VI. In addition, this series includes history and criticism of drama, as well as examinations of technique.

Early History of Travel & Geography

Offering a fascinating view into the perception of the world during the sixteenth and seventeenth centuries, this collection includes accounts of Columbus's discovery of the Americas and encompasses most of the Age of Discovery, during which Europeans and their descendants intensively explored and mapped the world. This series is a wealth of information from some the most groundbreaking explorers.

Early Fables & Fairy Tales

This series includes many translations, some illustrated, of some of the most well-known mythologies of today, including Aesop's Fables and English fairy tales, as well as many Greek, Latin and even Oriental parables and criticism and interpretation on the subject.

Early Documents of Language & Linguistics

The evolution of English and foreign languages is documented in these original texts studying and recording early philology from the study of a variety of languages including Greek, Latin and Chinese, as well as multilingual volumes, to current slang and obscure words. Translations from Latin, Hebrew and Aramaic, grammar treatises and even dictionaries and guides to translation make this collection rich in cultures from around the world.

Early History of the Law

With extensive collections of land tenure and business law "forms" in Great Britain, this is a comprehensive resource for all kinds of early English legal precedents from feudal to constitutional law, Jewish and Jesuit law, laws about public finance to food supply and forestry, and even "immoral conditions." An abundance of law dictionaries, philosophy and history and criticism completes this series.

Early History of Kings, Queens and Royalty

This collection includes debates on the divine right of kings, royal statutes and proclamations, and political ballads and songs as related to a number of English kings and queens, with notable concentrations on foreign rulers King Louis IX and King Louis XIV of France, and King Philip II of Spain. Writings on ancient rulers and royal tradition focus on Scottish and Roman kings, Cleopatra and the Biblical kings Nebuchadnezzar and Solomon.

Early History of Love, Marriage & Sex

Human relationships intrigued and baffled thinkers and writers well before the postmodern age of psychology and self-help. Now readers can access the insights and intricacies of Anglo-Saxon interactions in sex and love, marriage and politics, and the truth that lies somewhere in between action and thought.

Early History of Medicine, Health & Disease

This series includes fascinating studies on the human brain from as early as the 16th century, as well as early studies on the physiological effects of tobacco use. Anatomy texts, medical treatises and wound treatment are also discussed, revealing the exponential development of medical theory and practice over more than two hundred years.

Early History of Logic, Science and Math

The "hard sciences" developed exponentially during the 16th and 17th centuries, both relying upon centuries of tradition and adding to the foundation of modern application, as is evidenced by this extensive collection. This is a rich collection of practical mathematics as applied to business, carpentry and geography as well as explorations of mathematical instruments and arithmetic; logic and logicians such as Aristotle and Socrates; and a number of scientific disciplines from natural history to physics.

Early History of Military, War and Weaponry

Any professional or amateur student of war will thrill at the untold riches in this collection of war theory and practice in the early Western World. The Age of Discovery and Enlightenment was also a time of great political and religious unrest, revealed in accounts of conflicts such as the Wars of the Roses.

Early History of Food

This collection combines the commercial aspects of food handling, preservation and supply to the more specific aspects of canning and preserving, meat carving, brewing beer and even candy-making with fruits and flowers, with a large resource of cookery and recipe books. Not to be forgotten is a "the great eater of Kent," a study in food habits.

Early History of Religion

From the beginning of recorded history we have looked to the heavens for inspiration and guidance. In these early religious documents, sermons, and pamphlets, we see the spiritual impact on the lives of both royalty and the commoner. We also get insights into a clergy that was growing ever more powerful as a political force. This is one of the world's largest collections of religious works of this type, revealing much about our interpretation of the modern church and spirituality.

Early Social Customs

Social customs, human interaction and leisure are the driving force of any culture. These unique and quirky works give us a glimpse of interesting aspects of day-to-day life as it existed in an earlier time. With books on games, sports, traditions, festivals, and hobbies it is one of the most fascinating collections in the series.

The BiblioLife Network

This project was made possible in part by the BiblioLife Network (BLN), a project aimed at addressing some of the huge challenges facing book preservationists around the world. The BLN includes libraries, library networks, archives, subject matter experts, online communities and library service providers. We believe every book ever published should be available as a high-quality print reproduction; printed on-demand anywhere in the world. This insures the ongoing accessibility of the content and helps generate sustainable revenue for the libraries and organizations that work to preserve these important materials.

The following book is in the "public domain" and represents an authentic reproduction of the text as printed by the original publisher. While we have attempted to accurately maintain the integrity of the original work, there are sometimes problems with the original work or the micro-film from which the books were digitized. This can result in minor errors in reproduction. Possible imperfections include missing and blurred pages, poor pictures, markings and other reproduction issues beyond our control. Because this work is culturally important, we have made it available as part of our commitment to protecting, preserving, and promoting the world's literature.

GUIDE TO FOLD-OUTS MAPS and OVERSIZED IMAGES

The book you are reading was digitized from microfilm captured over the past thirty to forty years. Years after the creation of the original microfilm, the book was converted to digital files and made available in an online database.

In an online database, page images do not need to conform to the size restrictions found in a printed book. When converting these images back into a printed bound book, the page sizes are standardized in ways that maintain the detail of the original. For large images, such as fold-out maps, the original page image is split into two or more pages

Guidelines used to determine how to split the page image follows:

- Some images are split vertically; large images require vertical and horizontal splits.
- For horizontal splits, the content is split left to right.
- For vertical splits, the content is split from top to bottom.
- For both vertical and horizontal splits, the image is processed from top left to bottom right.

A DECLARATION OF THE TRVE manner of knowing *Christ Crucified.*

Galat. 6. 14.

God forbid that I should rei[oyce] but in the Crosse of our Lor[d] Iesus Christ, &c.

Printed at London by IOHN LEGATE Printer to the *Vniuersitie of Cambridge.* 1611.

And are to be sold in Pauls Church-yard at the signe of the Crowne by *Simon Waterson.*

To the Reader.

IT is the common sinne of men at this day, and that in the very places of learning, that Christ crucified *is not* known as he ought. The right knowledge of whome, is not to make often mention of his death and passion, and to call him our *Saviour*, or to handle the whole mysterie of *God incarnate* soundly and learnedly, though that be a worthy gift of God: but first of all, by the consideration of the passion to be touched with an inward and a liuely feeling of our sinnes, for which our Redeemer suffered the pangs of hell, and to growe to a through dislike of our selues & our liues past for them, and from the ground of the heart to purpose a reformation and a conformitie with Christ in all good duties

To the Reader.

ties that concerne man: secondly, in the passion, as in a myrror, to behold, and in beholding to labour to comprehend the length, the breadth, the height, the depth of the loue of the father that gaue his own deere son to death, & the goodnesse of the son that loued his enemies more then himselfe, that our hearts might bee rooted and grounded in the same loue, and bee further inflamed to loue God againe.

To further this true manner of knowing Christ crucifyed, I haue penned these few lines, read them at thy leisure, and haue care to put them in practise: otherwise thou art but an enemie of the crosse of Christ, though thou professe his name neuer so much.

Ian. 3. 1506.

W. Perkins.

OF THE
right knowledge of *Christ crucified.*

IT is the most excellent and worthy part of diuine wisedome to know Christ crucified. The Prophet *Esay* saith, *The knowledge of thy righteous seruant,* that is, Christ crucified, *shall iustifie many.* And Christ himselfe saith, *This is life eternall to know thee the only God, and whom thou hast sent Iesus Christ.* And Paul saith, *I haue decreed to know nothing among you, but Iesus Christ and him crucified.* Againe, *God forbid that I should reioyce in a-*

Esa. 53. 11.

Ioh. 17. 2.

2. Cor. 2. 1.

of Christ crucified. 3
ny thing but in the crosse *of our* Gal.6,14.
Lord Iesus Christ. Againe, I Phil.3.5;
thinke all things but losse *for
the excellent knowledge sake of
Christ Iesus my Lord, and doe
iudge them but dung, that I
might* winne *Christ.*

In the right way of knowing *Christ crucified* two points must bee considered; one, how Man for his part is to knowe Christ; the other, how hee is to be knowne of man.

Touching the first; Man must know Christ, not generally and confusedly, but by a liuely, powerfull, and operatiue *knowledge*: for otherwise the diuells themselues know Christ.

In this *knowledge* three things are required. The first is *notice or consideration,* whereby thou must conceiue in

A 3   minde

Of the right knowledge minde, vnderstand, and seririously bethinke thy selfe of Christ as he is reueyled in the history of the Gospel, & as he is offered to thy *particular person* in the ministerie of the word and Sacraments. And that this consideration may not bee dead and idle in thee, two things must be done: first thou must labour to feele thy selfe to *stand in need* of Christ crucified, yea to stand in excessiue neede euen of the very least drop of his bloud, for the washing away of thy sins. And vnlesse thou throughly feelest thy selfe to *want* all that goodnesse and grace that is in Christ, and that thou euen standest in extreame neede of his passion, thou shalt neuer learne or teach Christ in deed and truth. The second thing

is

is, with the vnderstanding of the doctrine of Christ to ioine thirsting, whereby man in his very soule and spirit longs after the participation of Christ, and saith in this case, as *Sampson* said, *Giue mee water, I die for thirst*.

The second part of knowledge is *application*, whereby thou must know and beleeue not onely that Christ was crucified, but that he was crucified for *thee*; for *thee*, I say, in particular. Here two rules must be remembred and practised: one, that Christ on the crosse was *thy* pledge and suretie in particular, that he then stood in the very roome and place in which thou thy selfe in thine owne person shouldst haue stood: that thy very personall and particular sinnes

Of the right knowledge 6

were imputed and applyed to him, that he stood guiltie, as a malefactour for them, and suffered the very pangs of hell, and that his sufferings are as much in acceptation with God, as if thou haddest borne the curse of the law in thine owne person eternally. The holding and beleeuing of this point is the very foundation of religion, as also of the Church of God. Therfore in any wise be carefull to apply Christ crucified to thy selfe: and *Elizeus* when he would reuiue the child of the Shunamite, went vp and lay vpon him, and put his mouth vpō his mouth, & his hands vpon his hands, & his eyes vpon his eyes, and stretched himselfe vpon him: euen so, if thou wouldst be reuiued

a. Kin. 4. 34.

uiued to euerlasting life, thou must by faith as it were set thy selfe vppon the crosse of Christ, and apply thy hands to his hands, thy feete to his feete, and thy sinnefull heart to his bleeding heart, and content not thy selfe with *Thomas* to put thy finger into his side, but euen diue and plunge thy selfe wholly both bodie and soule into the wounds and bloud of Christ. This will make thee to cry with *Thomas*, and say, *My Lord, my God*, and this is to be crucified *with Christ*. And yet doe not content thy selfe with this, but by faith also descend with Christ from the crosse to the graue, and bury thy selfe in the very buriall of Christ: and then looke as the dead soldier tumbled into the graue

8   Of the right knowledge

grave of *Elizeus* was made aliue at the very touching of his bodie; so shalt thou by a spirituall touching of Christ dead and buried, be quickned to life euerlasting. The second rule is, that Christ crucified *is thine*, being really giuen thee of God the father, euen as truely as houses and land are giuen or earthly fathers to their children: this thou must firmely hold and beleeue; and hence is it that the benefits of Christ are before God ours indeede for our iustification and saluation.

The third point in liuely knowledge is, that by all the *affections* of our hearts wee must be carried to Christ, and as it were transformed into him. Whereas he gaue himselfe wholy for vs, we can doe

no

2.Kin.13.21.

no lesse then bestowe our hearts vpon him. We must therefore labour aboue all, following the Martyr *Ignatius*, who said that Christ, *his loue was crucified.* We must value him at so high a price, that he must be vnto vs better then ten thousand worldes: yea all things which we enioy must be but as *drosse and dung* vnto vs in respect of him. Lastly, all our ioy, reioycing, comfort, and confidence must be placed in him. And that thus much is requisit in knowledge, it appeares by the common rule of expoundinge Scripture, that *words of knowledge implie affection.* And indeede it is but a knowledge swimming in the braine, which doth not alter and dispose the affections and the whole

whole man.

Thus much of our knowledge. Now followes the second point, how Christ is to bee knowne, hee must not bee known barely as god, or as mā, or as a Iew born in the tribe of Iudah, or as a terrible and iust iudge, but as hee is our *redeemer* and the very *price* of our redemption: and in this respect hee must bee considered as the common *Treasurie* and *store-house* of Gods Church, as *Paul* testifieth when hee saith, *In him are* all *the treasures of knowledge and wisedome hid*: and againe, *Blessed bee God, which hath blessed vs with all spirituall blessings in Christ*. And S. Iohn saith, that *of his fulnesse we receiue grace for grace*, Here then let vs marke that all the blessings of God, whether
spirituall

of Christ crucified.   11

spirituall or temporall, all I say, without exception are conueied vnto vs from the Father by Christ: and so they must be receiued of vs and no otherwise. That this point may bee further cleared, the benefits which wee receiue from Christ are to bee handled, and the manner of knowing them, The benefits of Christ are three, his *Merit*, his *Vertue*, his *Example*.

The *merit* of Christ, is the *value* and *price* of his death & passion, whereby any man is perfectly reconciled to God. This reconciltation hath two parts, *Remission* of sinnes, and *acceptation* to life euerlasting. Remission of sinnes, is the remoouing, or the abolishing both of the *guilt* and *punishment* of mans sinnes. By *guilt*

Vn-

I vnderstand a *subiection* or *obligation* to punishment, according to the order of diuine iustice. And the punishment of sinne is the *malediction* or *curse* of the whole lawe, which is the suffering of the first and second death. *Acceptation* to life euerlasting, is a giuing of right and title to the kingdome of heauen, and that for the merit of Chrifts obedience imputed. Nowe this benefit of reconciliation must bee knowne not by conceit and imagination, nor by carnall presumption; but by the inward testimonie of *Gods spirit* certifying our consciences thereof, which for this cause is called the *spirit of Reuelation*. And that we may attaine to infallible assurance of this benefit, we must call to minde

of Christ crucified.

minde the promises of the gospell touching remission of sinnes and life euerlasting: this beeing done, we must further *striue* and indeauour by the assurance of Gods spirit to apply them to our selues, and to beleeue that they belong vnto vs; and we must also put our selues often to all the exercises of inuocation and true repentance. For in and by our crying vnto heauen to God for reconciliation, comes the assurance thereof, as Scripture and Christian experience makes manifest. And if it so fall out, that any man in temptation apprehend and feele nothing but the furious indignation and wrath of God, against all reason and feeling he must hold to the merit of Christ, and know a
point

Of the right knowledge point of religion hard to bee learned, that God is a most louing father to them that haue care to serue him euen at that instant when hee shewes himselfe a most fierce and terrible enemie.

From the benefit of *reconciliation* proceede foure benefits. First, that excellent *peace of God* that passeth all vnderstanding, which hath sixe parts. The first is, *peace* with God and the blessed Trinitie. Rom. 5. 1. *Beeing iustified wee haue peace with God.* The second, *peace* with the good angels, Ioh. 1. 51. *Yee shall see the Angels of God ascending and descending vpon the sonne of man.* And that angels like armies of souldiers in campe about the seruants of God, and as nources bare
them

of Christ crucified.

them in their armes that they be neither hurt by the diuell and his angels, nor by his instruments, it proceeds of this that they beeing in Christ are partakers of his merits. The third is, *peace* with all such as feare God, & beleue in Christ. This *Esai* foretold when hee said, that the *woolfe shall dwell with the lambe, and the Leopard with the kidde, and the calfe and the Lyon and a fatte beast togither, and that a little child should lead them, &c.* 11. v. 6. The fourth is, *peace* with a mans owne selfe, when the conscience washed in the blood of Christ, ceaseth to accuse and terrifie: and when the will, affections, and inclinations of the whole man are obedient to the minde enlightned by the spirit & word of God, Coloss.

loss. 3. *Let the peace of God rule in your hearts.* The fift is *peace* with enemies, and that two waies. First, in that such as beleeue in Christ, seeke to haue peace with all men, hurting none but doing good to all: secondly, in that God restraines the malice of the enemies: and inclines their hearts to bee peaceable. Thus God brought Daniel *into loue and fauour with the chiefe of the Eunuches.* The last is, *peace with* all creatures in heauen and earth, in that they serue for mans saluation Psa.91.13. *Thou shalt walke vpon the lyon and the aspe: the young lyon and the dragon shalt thou* tread *vnderfoote.* Hos.2.18. *And in that day will I make* a couenant *for them with the beasts of the field, and with the foules of heauen.*
Now

Chap.1.9.

Of Christ crucified. 17

Nowe this benefit of peace is knowne partly by the testimonie of the spirit, and partly by a daily experience thereof.

The second benefit is a *recouerie* of that *right and title*, which man ~~hath~~ to all creatures in heauen and earth, and all temporall blessings; which right *Adam* lost to himselfe and euery one of his posteritie. 1.Cor.3.22. *Whether it bee the world, or life, or death: whether they bee things present, or things to come,* all *are yours*. Now the right way of knowing this one benefit is this: Whē God vouchsafeth meat, drinke, apparell, houses, lands, &c. wee must not barely consider them as blessings of God, for that very heathen men, which know not God, can doe; but wee must acknowknowledge and esteeme them as blessings proceeding from the speciall loue of God the father, whereby hee loues vs in Christ; and procured vnto vs by the merit of Christ crucified: and wee must labour in this point to be setled & perswaded: and so oft as wee see and vse the creatures of God for our owne benefit, this point should come to our mindes. Blessings conceiued apart from Christ are misconceiued: whatsoeuer they are in themselues, they are no blessings to vs but in and by Christs merit. Therefore this order must bee obserued touching earthly blessings: first wee must haue part in the merit of Christ, and then secondly by meanes of that merit, aright before God and com-

comfortable vse of the things wee enioy. All men that haue and vse the creatures of God otherwise as gifts of God but not by Christ, vse them but as flat *vsurpers* & theeues. For this cause it is not sufficient for vs generally and confusedly to knowe Christ to bee our redeemer; but wee must learne to see, knowe, and acknowledge him in euery particular gift & blessing of God. If men vsing the creatures of meate and drinke, could, when they behold them, with all by the eie of faith behold in them the merit of Christs passion, there would not bee so much excesse and riot, so much surfetting and drunkennesse, as there is: and if men could consider their houses & lands, &c. as blessings to them, and

that

that by the fountaine of blessing the *merits* of Christ, there should not bee so much fraud and deceit, so much iniustice, and oppression in bargaining as there is.

That which I haue nowe said of meates, drinkes, apparell, must likewise bee vnderstood of gentrie and nobility, in as much as noble birth without new birth in Christ is but an earthly vanitie: the like may bee said of physicke, sleepe, health, libertie, yea of the very breathing in the aire. And to goe yet further: in our recreations Christ must be knowne. For all recreation stands in the vse of things indifferent, and the holy vse of all things indifferent, is purchased vnto vs by the blood of Christ. For this cause it is very meete that Christian

Consider Coloss. 3, 11 and 2, 10.

men and women should with their earthly recreations ioyn spirituall meditation of the death of Christ, and from the one take occasion to bethinke themselues of the other. If this were practised, ther should not be so many vnlawfull sports & delights, & so much abuse of lawfull recreation as there is.

The third benefit is, that all crosses, afflictions, and iudgements whatsoeuer, cease to be curses and punishments to them that are in Christ; and are onely meanes of *correction* or *triall*; because his death hath také away not some fewe parts, but all and euery part of the curse of the whole law. Now in all *crosses*, Christ is to be knowne of vs on this manner. We must iudge of our afflictions as chastisments or trials,

trials, proceeding not from reuenging iudge, but from the hand of a bountifull and louing father; and therefore they must be conceiued in & with the merit of Christ: and if wee doe otherwise regard them, we take them as curses and punishments of sinne. And hence it followes that subiection to Gods hand in *all crosses*, is a marke and badge of the true Church.

The last benefit is, that death is properly no death, but a rest or sleepe. Death, therfore must be knowne and considered not as it is set forth in the lawe, but as it is altered and changed by the death of Christ: & when death comes, wee must then looke vpon it through Christs death, as through a glasse: and thus it will

will appeare to be but a passage from this life to euerlasting life.

Thus much of the *merit* of Christ crucified. Now followes his *vertue* which is the power of his godhead, whereby he creates newe hearts in all them that beleeue in him, and makes them new creatures. This vertue is double: the first is the *power of his death*, whereby he freed himselfe from the punishment & imputation of our sinnes: and the same vertue serueth to mortifie and crucifie the corruptions of our mindes, wills, affections, euen as a corasiue doth wast and consume the rotten and dead flesh in any part of mans bodie.

The second, is the *vertue of Christs resurrection*, which is also the power of his Godhead, whereby hee raised himselfe from death to life: and the very same power serueth to raise those that belong to Christ, from their sinnes in this life, and from the graue in the day of the last iudgement. Now the knowledge of this double vertue must not bee onely speculatiue, that is, barely conceiued in the braine, but it must bee experimentall: because wee ought to haue experience of it in our hearts & liues: and wee should labour by all meanes possible to feele the power of Christs death killing and mortifying our sinnes, and the vertue of his resurrection in the putting of spirituall life into vs, that wee might bee able to say that wee liue not, but that Christ

of Christ crucified.

Christ liues in vs. This was one of the most excellent and principall things which *Paul* sought for, who saith, *I haue counted all things* losse *and doe iudge them to bee* dung, *that I may* know *him and the vertue of his resurrection.* Phil. 3.10. And hee saith that this is the right way to know and learne Christ, *to cast off the olde man, which is corrupt through the deceiuable lusts, and to put on the new man which is created in righteousnesse and true holinesse,* Eph. 4.24.

The third benefit is *the example* of Christ. We deceiue our selues, if we thinke that he is onely to bee knowne of vs as a Redeemer, and not as a *spectacle* or *patterne* of al good duties, to which wee ought to conforme our selues. Good men

men indeede, that haue beene or in the present are vpon the earth the seruants of God, must bee followed of vs: but they must bee followed no otherwise then they followe Christ, and Christ must be followed in the practise of euery good duty that may concerne vs without exception simply and absolutely, 1. Cor. 11.1.

Our conformitie with Christ standes either in the framing of our inward and spirituall life, or in the practise of outward and morall duties.

Conformitie of spirituall life is, not by doing that which Christ did vpon the crosse & afterward, but a doing of the like by a certaine kind of imitation. And it hath foure parts. The first is, a *Spirituall oblation.*

oblation. For as Christ in the garden & vpon the crosse, by prayer made with strong cries & teares, presented & resigned himselfe to bee a sacrifice of propitiation to the iustice of his Father for mans sinne: so must we also in prayer present and resigne our selues, our soules, our bodies, our vnderstanding, will, memorie, affections, and all we haue to the seruice of God, in the generall calling of a Christian, and in the particular callings in which hee hath placed vs. Take an example in *Dauid, Sacrifice* & *burnt offering* (saith he) *thou wouldest not, but eares thou hast pierced vnto mee, then said I, loe I come: I desire to doe thy will, O God, yea thy lawe is within my heart,* Psal. 40. 7.

The second is, *conformitie in the crosse* two waies. For first, as hee bare his owne crosse to the place of execution: so must wee as good disciples of Christ deny our selues, take vp all the crosses and afflictions that the hand of God shal lay vpon vs. Againe, wee must become like vnto him in the crucifying and mortifying the masse and bodie of sinne which wee carie about vs. Gal. 5.24. *They which are Christs haue crucified the flesh with the affections and lusts thereof.* Wee must doe as the Iewes did, wee must set vp the crosses and gybbets whereon wee are to fasten and hang this flesh of ours, that is, the sinne and corruption that cleaues and stickes vnto vs, and by the sword of the spirit wound it euen

euen to death. This beeing done, we must yet go further, and labour by experience to see and feele the very death of it, and to lay it as it were in a graue neuer to rise againe: and therefore we should daily cast new moulds vpon it. The third is, *a spirituall resurrection*, whereby we should by Gods grace vse meanes that we may euery day more and more come out of our sinnes, as out of a loathsome graue; to liue vnto God in newnesse of life, as Christ rose from his graue. And because it is an hard matter for a man to come out of the graue or rather dungeon of his sinnes, this worke cannot be done at once but by degrees, as God shall giue grace. Considering we lie by nature dead in our sinnes,

sinnes, and stinke in them as loathsome carion, first wee must beginne to stirre our selues as a man that comes out of a swowne, awakened by the word and voice of Christ sounding in our deafe eares; secondly, we must raise vp our minds to a better state and condition as wee vse to raise vp our bodies: after this wee must put out of the graue first one hand, then the other. This done, wee must doe our indeauour as it were vpon our knees, at the least to put one foote out of this sepulchre of sinne, the rather when wee see our selues to haue one foot of the bodie in the graue of the earth, that in the day of iudgement we may bee wholy deliuered from all bondes of corruption. The fourth part

part is, a *spirituall ascension* into heauen, by a continual eleuation of the heart & minde to Christ sitting at the right hand of the Father, as *Paul* saith, *Haue your conuersation in heauen:* and, *If ye be risen with Christ, seeke things that are aboue.*

Conformitie in morall duties, is either generall or speciall. Generall, is to be holy as he is holy. Rom. 8. 29. *Those whome he knew before he hath predestinate to be* like the image *of his Sonne*, that is, not onely in the crosse, but also in holines and glorie, 1. Ioh. 3. *He which hath this hope purifieth himselfe* euen as hee is pure.

Speciall conformitie, is chiefly in foure vertues; Faith, Loue, Meekenes, Humilitie. We

Wee must bee like him in faith. For as hee, when hee apprehended the wrath of God and the very pangs of hell were vpon him, wholly stayed himselfe vpon the aide, helpe, protection, and good pleasure of his Father, euen to the last: so must wee by a true and liuely faith depend wholly on Gods mercie in Christ, as it were with both our hands, in peace, in trouble, in life, and in the very pang of death: and wee must not in any wise let our hold goe; no, though wee should feele our selues descend to hell.

Wee must bee like him in meekenesse. Matth. 11.u.28. *Learne of mee that am meeke and lowly.* His meekenesse shewed it selfe in the patient bearing of all iniuries and abuses

of Christ crucified.

buses offered by the hands of sinnefull and wretched men, and in the suffering of the curse of the lawe, without grudging or repining, and with submission to his fathers will in all things. Nowe the more wee follow him herein, the more shall wee bee *conformable* to him in his death and passion, *Phil.* 3. 10.

Thirdly, hee must bee our example in *Loue*: he loued his enemies more then himselfe. Eph. 5. 4. *Walke in loue euen as Christ loued vs, and hath giuen himselfe for vs an oblation and sacrifice of sweete smelling sauour vnto God.* The like loue ought wee to shew, by doing seruice to all mē in the cōpasse of our callings, and by beeing all things to all men (as *Paul* was) that wee might doe them all

all the good wee can both for bodie and soule, 1. Cor. 9. 19.

Lastly, wee must followe Christ in *humilitie*, whereof hee is a wonderfull spectacle, in that being God, he became man for vs: and of a man became a worme that is troden vnder foote, that hee might saue man. Phil. 2. 5. *Let the same minde bee in you that was in Iesus Christ, who beeing in the forme of God, humbled himselfe and became obedient to the death, euen to the death of the crosse.*

And here we must obserue that the *example* of Christ hath somthing more in it then any other example hath or can haue: for it doth not onely shew vs what wee ought to doe (as the examples of other men doe) but it is a *remedie* against

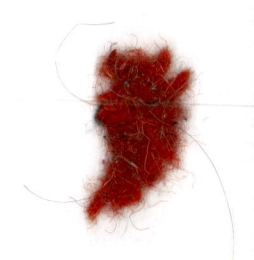

against many vices, and a *motiue* to many good duties. First of all the serious consideration of this, that the very Sonne of God himselfe suffered all the paines and tormēts of hell on the crosse for our sinnes, is the proper and most effectuall meanes to stirre vp our hearts to a godly sorrow for them. And that this thing may come to passe, euery man must bee setled without doubt, that hee was the man that crucified Christ; that he is to bee blamed as well as *Iudas*, *Herod*, *Pontius Pilate*, and the Iewes: and that his sinnes should bee the nayles, the speares, and the thornes, that pierced him. When this meditation beginnes to take place, bitternes of spirit with wailing and mourning takes place

place in like manner. *Zach. 12. 10. And they shall looke vpon him whome they haue pearced, and they shall lament for him as one lamenteth for his onely sonne.* Peter in his first sermon strooke the Iewes as with a thunder-clap from heauen when hee said vnto them, *Ye haue* crucified *the Lord of glorie,* so as the same time three thousand men were pricked in their hearts, and saide, *Men and brethren, what shall wee doe to bee saued?* Againe, if Christ for our sins shedde his heart blood: and if our sinnes made him sweate water & blood, oh then why should not wee our selues shedde bitter teares, and why should not our hearts bleede for them? He that findes himselfe so dull and hardened
that

that the paſſion of Chriſt doth not humble him, is in a lamentable caſe, for there is no faith in the death of Chriſt, effectuall in him as yet.

Secondly, the meditation of the paſſion of Chriſt is a moſt notable meanes to breed repentance and reformation of life in time to come. For when wee begin to thinke that Chriſt crucified, by ſuffering, the firſt and ſecond death, hath procured vnto vs remiſſion of all our ſinnes paſt, and freed vs from hell, death, and damnation: then, if there bee but a ſparke of grace in vs, wee begin to be of another minde, and to reaſon thus with our ſelues: What? hath the Lord binne thus mercifull vnto me, that am in my ſelfe but a firebrand of hell, as to free me frō de-

deserued destruction and to receiue me to fauour in Christ? yea, no doubt he hath, his name be blessed therefore: I will not therefore sinne any more as I haue done, but rather indeauour hereafter to keepe my selfe from euery euill way. And thus faith purifies both heart and life.

Thirdly, when thou art in any paine of body or sicknes, thinke how light these are. cōpared to the agony and bloodie sweat, to the crowne of thornes and nailes of Christ. When thou art wronged in word or deede by any man, turne thine eie to the crosse, consider how meekely he suffered all abuses for the most part in silence and praied for them that crucified him.

When

of Christ crucified.

When thou art tempted with pride or vaine-glorie, consider how for *thy* proper sinne Christ was despised and mocked and condemned among theeues. When anger and desire of reuenge inflame thine heart, think how Christ gaue himselfe to death to saue his enemies, euen then when they did most cruelly intreat him, and shed his blood: and by these meditations, specially if they be mingled with faith, thy minde shall be eased.

Thus we see howe *Christ crucified* is to be knowne: and hence ariseth a threefolde knowledge: one of God, the second of our neighbours, the third of our selues.

Touching the first, if we would knowe the true God aright, and know him to our sal-

saluation, wee must knowe him onely in *Christ crucified.* God in himselfe and his owne maiestie is inuisible, not onely to the eyes of the bodie, but also to the very minds of men, and hee is reuealed to vs onely in Christ, in whome hee is to bee seene as in a glasse. For in Christ hee setteth forth and giues his iustice, goodnesse, wisedome, & himselfe wholly vnto vs. For this cause he is called the *brightnesse of the glorie and the ingrauen* forme of *the person of the father.* Heb. 1. 3. *and the* image *of the inuisible God,* Coloss. 1. 15. Therefore wee must not know God and seeke him any where else but in Christ: and whatsoeuer out of Christ comes vnto vs in the name of God, is a fla idol of mans braine.

As for our neighbours, those especially that are of Chrifts Church, they are to be knowne of vs on this manner: Whē we are to do any dutie vnto them, wee muft not barely refpect their perfons, but *Chrift crucified* in them, and them in Chrift. When *Paul* perfecuted fuch as called on the name of Chrift, he then from heauen cried, *Saul, Saul, why perfecuteft thou mee?* Here then let this be marked, that when the poore comes to vs for reliefe, it is Chrift that comes to our dores, and faith, I am hungrie, I am thirftie, I am naked: & let the bowels of compaffion bee in vs towards them as towardes Chrift, vnleffe wee will heare that fearefulfentēce in the day of iudgement, *Goe ye curfed into*

into hell, &c. I was hungrie, and ye fed me not: I was naked, and ye did not cloath me, &c.

Thirdly, the right knowledge of our selues ariseth of the knowledge of *Christ crucified*, in whome and by whome wee come to know fiue speciall things of our selues. The first, how grieuous our sinnes are, and therefore how miserable wee are in regard of them. If wee consider our offences in themselues, and as they are in vs, wee may soone bee deceiued because the conscience being corrupted often erreth in giuing testimonie, and by that meanes maketh sinne to appeare lesse then it is indeede. But if sinne bee considered in the death & passion of Christ, whereof it was the cause, and the vilenes thereof measure by the vnspeakable torments endured by the sonne of God, and if the greatnesse of the offence of man bee esteemed by the endlesse satisfaction made to the iustice of God, the least sinne that is will appeare to bee a sinne indeede, and that most grieuous and ougly. Therefore *Christ crucified* must bee vsed of vs as a myrrour or looking-glasse, in which wee may fully take a view of our wretchednesse and miserie, and what wee are by nature. For such as the passion of Christ was in the eies of men, such is our passion or conditiō in the eies of God: & that which wicked men did to Christ, the same doth sinne and *Satan* to our very soules.

The second point is, that men beleeuing in Christ are
not

not their owne, or Lords of themselues, but wholly both body and soule belong to Christ, in that they were giuen to him of God the father, and hee hath purchased them with his owne blood. 1.Cor.3, *Ye are Christs, and Christ Gods.* Hence it commeth to passe (which is not to be forgotten) that Christ esteemeth all the crosses and afflictions of his people, as his owne proper afflictions. Hence again we must learne to giue vp our selues both in body and soule to the honour and seruice of Christ, whose we are.

The third is, that euery true beleeuer, not as hee is *a man*, but as hee is *a new man*, or a Christian, hath his beeing and subsisting from Christ, *We are members of his bodie, of his*

his flesh, and of his bone, Eph. 5. 30. In which words, *Paul* aludes to the speech of *Adam*, Gen. 3. *Thou art bone of my bone, and flesh of my flesh*, and thereby hee teacheth, that as *Eue* was made of a ribbe taken out of the side of *Adam*; so doth the whole Church of God and euery man regenerate, spring and arise out of the blood that streamed from the heart and side of Christ crucified.

The fourth is, that all good workes done of vs, proceede from the vertue and merit of *Christ crucified*, hee is the cause of them in vs, and wee are the causes of them in and by him. *Without me* (saith he) *ye can doe nothing*: and, *Euery branch that beareth no fruit in mee*, marke well hee saith, in mee, *he taketh away*, a way. Ioh. 15. 2.

The fifth point is, that we owe vnto Christ an endlesse dept. For he was crucified onely as our surety & pledge, & in the spectacle of his passion we must consider our selues as the chiefe debters, & that the very discharge of our dept, that is, the sinnes which are inherent in vs, were the proper cause of all the endles paines and torments that Christ endured, that he might set vs most miserable bankerupts at libertie from hell, death, and damnation. For this his vnspeakable goodnes, if we doe but once thinke of it seriously, we must needes confesse that we owe our selues, our soules, and bodies, and all that we haue as a debt due vnto him. And so soone

as

as any man beginnes to know *Christ crucified*, hee knowes his owne debt, and thinkes of the payment of it.

Thus we see how Christ is to bee knowne: now wee shall not neede to make much examination, whether this manner of knowing and acknowledging of Christ, take any place in the world or no: for fewe there bee that knowe him as they ought. The Turke euen at this very day knowes him not, but as a Prophet. The Iew scorneth his *crosse* and *passion*. The Popish churches, though in word they confesse him, yet doe they not knowe him as they ought. The Friers and Iesuits in their sermons at this day commonly vse the Passion, as a meanes to stirre vp pitie and compassion

48   *Of the right knowledge*
paſſion towards Chriſt, who
beeing ſo righteous a man
was ſo hardly entreated, and
to inflame their hearts to an
hatred of the Iewes, and *Iudas*, and *Pontius Pilate*, that
put our bleſſed Sauiour to
death; but all this may be
done in any other hiſtorie.
And the ſeruice of God
which in that Church ſtands
now in force by the Canon
of the Councell of Trent, de
faceth *Chriſt crucified*, in tha
the paſſions of martyrs ar
made meritorious, and the
very wood of the croſſe thei
onely helpe: and the virgin
Marie the *Queene of heauen*
and a *mother of mercie*; wh(
in remiſſion of ſinnes ma
commaund her ſonne: & the
giue religious adoration t(
dumbe crucifixes made b)

the

of Christ crucified.

the hand and arte of man.

The common Protestant likewise commeth short herein for three causes. First, whereas in word they acknowledge him to bee their Sauiour, that hath redeemed them from their euill conuersation, yet indeede they make him *a patrone of their sinnes*. The thiefe makes him the receiuer, the murderer makes him his refuge,(*b*) the adulterer (be it spoken with reuerence vnto his maiestie) makes him the baud. For generally men walk on in their euill waies, some liuing in this sin, some in that, and yet for all this, they perswade themselues that God is merciful, and that Christ hath freed them from death and damnation. Thus Christ that came to abolish sinne, is made

b Caluin. Gal.6.2.

a maina maintainer thereof, and the common pack-horse of the world to beare euery mans burden. Secondly, men are content to take knowledge of the merit of Christs passion for the remission of their sinnes, but in the meane season the vertue of Christs death in the mortifying of sinne, and the blessed example of his passion, which ought to be followed and expressed in our liues and conuersations, is little or nothing regarded. Thirdly, men vsually content themselues generally and confusedly to know Christ to be their redeemer, neuer once seeking in euery particular estate and condition of life, and in euery particular blessing of God, to feele the benefit of his passion.

What

What is the cause that almost all the world liue in securitie, neuer almost touched for their horrible sinnes? surely the reason is, because they did neuer yet seriously consider, that Christ in the garden lay groueling vpon the earth sweating water and bloud for their offences. Againe, all such as by fraud and oppression, or any kind of hard dealing, suck the bloud of poore men, neuer yet knew that their sinnes drew out the heart bloud of Christ. And proud men and women that are puffed vp by reason of their attire, which is the badge of their shame, and neuer cease hunting after strange fashions, doe not consider that Christ was not crucified in gay attire, but naked, that he might

Of the right knowledge might beare the whole shame and curse of the law for vs. These and such like, whatsoeuer they say in word, if wee respect the tenour of their liues, are flat enemies of the crosse of Christ, and tread his precious blood vnder their feete.

Now then, considering this so weightie and speciall a point of religion is so much neglected, O man or woman, high or low, young or olde, if thou haue beene wanting this way, beginne for very shame to learne, and learning truly to *know* Christ crucified. And that thou maiest attaine to this, behold him often, not in the wooden crucifix after the Popish manner, but in the preaching of the word, and in the Sacramēts, in which thou shalt see *him crucified* before thine eyes, *Gal.* 3. 1. Desire not here vpon earth to behold him with the bodily eie, but looke vpon him with the eie of true and liuely faith, applying him and his merites to thy selfe as thine owne, and that with broken and bruised heart, as the poore Israelites stung with fierie serpents euen to death, beheld the brasen serpent. Againe, thou must looke vpon him first of all as a *glasse or spectacle*, in which thou shalt see Gods glorie greater in thy redemption, then in thy creation. In the creation, appeared Gods infinite wisedome, power and goodnesse: in thy redemption by the passion of Christ, his endlesse iustice and mercy. In the creation, thou art a member of the first *Adam*, and bearest his image: in thy redemption thou art a member of the second *Adam*. In the first, thou art indued with naturall life, in the second, with spirituall. In the first, thou hast in the person of *Eue* thy beginning of the rib of *Adam*, in the second, thou hast thy beginning, as thou art borne of God out of the bloud of Christ. Lastly, in the first, God gaue life in commanding that to bee, which was not: in the second, hee giues life not by life, but by death, euen of his owne Sonne. This is the mysterie vnto which the Angels themselues desire to looke into. *1.Pet.1.12.* Secondly, thou must behold him as the full *price of thy* redemption, and perfect recōciliatiō with God; & pray earnestly to God, that he would seale vp the same in

thy

thy very conscience by his holy spirit. Thirdly, thou must behold Christ as an *example*, to whom thou must conform thy selfe by regeneration. For this cause giue diligence, that thou maist by experience say, that thou art dead, and crucified, and buried with Christ, and that thou risest againe with him to newnesse of life; that hee enlightens thy minde, and by degrees reformes thy will and affections, and giues thee both the will and the deede in euery good thing. and that thou maiest not faile in this thy knowledge, read the historie of Christs passion, obserue all the parts and circumstances therof, and apply them to thy selfe for thy full conuersion. When thou readest, that Christ went to the garden,

garden, as his custome was, where the Iewes might soonest attach him, consider that hee went to the death of the crosse for thy sinnes willingly and not of constraint; and that therefore thou for thy part shouldest doe him all seruice freely and franckly, *Psal.* 110. 3. When thou hearest that in his agony his soule was heauy vnto death, knowe it was for thy sins, and that thou shouldest much more conceiue heauinesse of heart for the same: againe, that this sorrow of his is ioy & reioycing vnto thee, if thou wilt beleeue in him; therefore *Paul* saith, I say againe, reioyce in the Lord. When thou readest that in the garden he prayed lying groueling on his face, sweating water and bloud, beginne to

to thinke seriously what an vnspeakable measure of Gods wrath was vpon thy blessed Sauiour, that did prostrate his body vpon the earth, and cause the bloud to follow; and thinke that thy sinnes must needes bee most hainous, that brought such bloudie & grieuous paines vpon him. Also thinke it a very shame for thee to carrie thy head to heauen with haughtie lookes, to wallow in thy pleasures, and to drawe the innocent bloud of thy poore brethren by oppression and deceit, for whom Christ sweat water and bloud; and take an occasion from Christs agonie, to lay aside the pride of thy heart, to be ashamed of thy selfe, to grieue in heart, yea euen to bleed for thine owne offences, casting
downe

downe and humbling thy selfe with *Ezra,* saying, O my God, I am confounded and ashamed to lift vp mine eies vnto thee, my God: for mine iniquities are increased, & my trespasse is growne vp into heauen, When thou readest that Christ was taken and bound, thinke that thy very sinnes brought him into the power of his enemies, and were the very bondes wherewith he was tyed: thinke that thou shouldest haue beene bound in the very same manner, vnlesse he had beene a surety and pledge for thee: thinke also that thou in the selfe same manner art bound and tyed with the chaines of thine owne sinnes, and that by nature thy will, affections, and whole spirit is tyed and chain-

chained to the will of the deuill, so as thou canst doe nothing but that which he willeth: lastly, thinke and beleeue that the bonds of Christ serue to purchase thy libertie from hell, death, and damnation. When thou hearest that he was brought before *Annas* and *Caiaphas*, thinke it was meete, that thy surety and pledge who was to suffer the condemnation due vnto thee, should by the high priest, as by the mouth of God, bee condemned: and wonder at this, that the very coessentiall and eternall sonne of God, euen the very soueraign iudge of the world, standes to be iudged, and that by wicked men; perswading thy selfe that this so great confusion comes of thy sinnes. Whereupon
bee-

beeing further amazed at thy fearefull estate, humble thy selfe in dust and ashes, & pray God so to soften thy stonie heart, that thou maiest turne to him, and by true faith lay hold on Christ, who hath thus exceedingly abased himselfe, that his ignominie may be thy glorie, and his arraignment thy perfect absolution. When thou readest that *Barrabas* the murderer was preferred before Christ, though hee exceeded both men and angels in holinesse; thinke it was to manifest his innocencie, and that thy very sins pulled vpon him this shamefull reproach; and in that for thy cause hee was esteemed worse then *Barrabas*, thinke of thy selfe as a most haynous and wretched sinner, and (as *Paul*

of Christ crucified.

Paul saith) the head of all sinners. When thou readest that hee was openly and iudicially condemned to the cursed death of the crosse, consider what is the wrath and furie of God against sinne, and what is his great and infinite mercy to sinners: and in this spectacle looke vpon thy selfe, and with groanes of heart crie out, and say, O good God, what settest thou here before mine eyes? I, euen I haue sinned, I am guiltie and worthie of damnation. Whence comes this chaunge, that thy blessed son is in my roome, but of thy vnspeakable mercie? Wretch that I am, how haue I forgotten my selfe, and thee also my God? O sonne of God, how long hast thou abased thy selfe for me? Therefore giue me me grace, O God, that beholding mine owne estate in the person of my Sauiour thus condemned, I may detest and loath my sinnes that are the cause thereof, and by a liuely faith imbrace that absolution which thou offerest mee in him, who was condemned in my stead and roome. O Iesu Christ Sauiour of the world, giue mee thy holy and blessed Spirit, that I may iudge my selfe, and bee as vile and base in mine owne eyes, as thou wast vile and base before the Iewes: also vnite mee vnto thee by the same spirit, that in thee I may be as worthy to be accepted before God, as I am worthy in my selfe to bee detested for my sinnes. When thou readest that hee was clad in purple and crowned with

thornes

of Christ crucified.

thornes, mocked and spitte vpon, behold the euerlasting shame that is due vnto thee, and bee ashamed of thy selfe, and in this point conforme thy selfe to Christ, and bee content (as hee was) to bee reproched, abused, and despised, so it bee for a good cause. When thou readest, that before his crucifying, hee was stript of all his cloathes, think it was, that hee beeing naked might bare thy shame on the crosse, and with his most precious and rich nakednesse couer thy deformitie. When thou readest the complaint of Christ, that hee was forsaken of his father, consider how hee suffered the pangs and torments of hell as thy pledge and suretie. Learne by his vnspeakable tormēts what a feare-

64 *Of the right knowledge*
a fearefull thing it is to sinne against God, and beginne to renounce thy selfe, and detest thy sins, & to walke as a childe of light, according to the measure of grace receiued. When thou commest to die, set before thine eies Christ in the middest of all his torments on the crosse: in beholding of which spectacle to thy endles comfort, thou shalt see a paradise in the middest of hell: God the Father reconciled vnto thee, thy Sauiour reaching out his hands vnto thee, to receiue thy soule vnto him, and his crosse as a ladder to aduance it to eternall glorie. Whereas he cried aloud with a strong voice at the point of death, it was to shew that hee died willingly, without violence or constraint from any

crea

of Christ crucified. 65

creature, and that if it had so pleased him, hee could haue freed himselfe from death, & haue cast his very enemies to the very bottome of hell. When thou readest that hee commended his soule into the hands of his father, consider that thy soule also (so be it thou wilt beleeue in him) is deliuered vp into the hands of God, and shall bee preserued against the rage and malice of all thine enemies, and hereupon thou maiest bee bolde to commend thy spirit into the hands of God the father. When thou readest of his death, consider that thy sinnes were the cause of it, and that thou shouldst haue suffered the same eternally, vnlesse the son of God had come in thy roome: againe, consider
by

his death as a ransome, and apprehend the same by faith, as the meanes of thy life: for by death Christ hath wounded both the first and second death, and hath made his crosse to be a throne or tribunall seate of iudgement against all his and thine enemies. When thou readest of the trembling of the earth at the death of Christ, thinke with thy self, it did in his kind, as it were, grone vnder the burden of the sinnes of men in the world: and by his motion then, it signified that euen thou and the rest deserued rather to be swallowed of the earth, and to goe downe into the pit aliue, then to haue any part in the merit of Christ crucified. When thou readest of his buriall, thinke that it was

was to ratifie his death, and to vanquish death euen in his owne denne. Apply this buriall to thy selfe, and beleeue that it serues to make thy graue a bedde of doune, and to free thy bodie from corruption. Lastly, pray to God that thou maiest feele the power of the spirit of Christ, weakning and consuming the bodie of sinne, euen as a dead corps rottes in the graue, till it be resolued to dust.

When thou hast thus perused and applyed to thy selfe the historie of the Passion of Christ, goe yet further, and labour by faith to see Christ crucified in all the workes of God, either in thee, or vpon thee. Behold him at thy table in meate and drinke, which is as it were a liuely sermon and
a dai-

a daily pleadge of the mercie of God in Christ. Behold him in all thine afflictions, as thy partner that pitieth thy case, and hath compassion on thee. Behold him in thy most daungerous temptations, in which the diuell thundreth damnation, behold him I say, as a mighty *Sampson* bearing away the gates of his enemies vpon his owne shoulders: and killing more by death then by life, crucifying the diuell, euen then when hee is crucified, by death killing death: by entrance into the graue, opening the graue and giuing life to the dead; and in the house of death spoiling him of all his strength and power. Behold him in all the afflictions of thy brethren, as though hee himselfe were naked, hungry, sicke

of Christ crucified. 69

sicke, harbourlesse, and do vnto them all the good thou canst, as to Christ himselfe. If thou wouldest behold God himselfe, looke vpon him in *Christ* crucified, who is the ingrauen image of the fathers person; and know it to be a terrible thing in the time of the trouble of thy conscience to think of God without Christ, in whose face the glorie of God in his endlesse mercie is to bee seene. 2. *Cor.* 4.6. If thou wouldest come to God for grace, for comfort, for saluation, for any blessing, come first to Christ hanging, bleeding, dying vpon the crosse, without whome there is no hearing God, no helping God, no sauing God, no God to thee at all. In a word, let Christ bee all things
with-

without exception vnto thee *Coloss.* 3. 11. for when thou praiest for any blessing either temporall or spirituall, be it whatsoeuer it will bee or can bee, thou must aske it at the hands of God the father, by the merit and mediation of Christ crucified: now looke as wee aske blessings at Gods hand, so must we receiue them of him; and as they are receiued, so must wee possesse and vse them daily, namely, as gifts of God procured to vs by the merit of Christ: which gifts for this very cause, must bee wholly imploied to the honour of Christ.

FINIS.

A Direction for the gouernment of the Tongue according to Gods word.

PRINTED BY IOHN LEGAT
Printer to the Vniuersitie of
Cambridge. 1603.

And are to be sold in Pauls Churchyard at the signe of the Crowne by Simon Waterson.

CPSIA information can be obtained at www.ICGtesting.com
Printed in the USA
LVOW03s2111110515

438055LV00016B/402/P